DISCOVERING ANCIENT TECHNOLOGY

DISCOVERING THE TECHNOLOGY OF ANCIENT EGYPT

LINDSEY LOWE

Cavendish Square

Published in 2024 by Cavendish Square Publishing, LLC
2544 Clinton Street, Buffalo, NY 14224

Portions of this work were originally authored by Charlie Samuels and published as *Technology in Ancient Egypt*. All new material this edition authored by Lindsey Lowe.

Website: cavendishsq.com

Children's Publisher: Anne O'Daly
Design Manager: Keith Davis
Designer: Lynne Lennon
Picture Manager: Sophie Mortimer

Picture Credits
Front Cover: iStock: domin_domin br; Shutterstock: GTS Productions t.
Public Domain: Jeff Dahl 38, Marie-Lan Nyuyen 33, Sharp Photography/Charles Sharp 6, Vassil 38, Walters Art Museum 39, 40; Shutterstock: Tawfik Deifalla 14, Kokhanchikov 28, PixiHound 31, Will Rogrigues 7, Nat Ulrich 4, Mikhail Zahranichny 24; Thinkstock: Dorling Kindersley RF 30, Ingram Publshing 36; istockphoto 4, 8, 12, 18, 22, 34; Photos.com 1, 5, 10, 15. 32.

Cataloging-in-Publication Data

Names: Lowe, Lindsey.
Title: Discovering the technology of ancient Egypt / Lindsey Lowe.
Description: Buffalo, New York : Cavendish Square Publishing, 2024. |
Series: Discovering ancient technology | Includes glossary and index.
Identifiers: ISBN 9781502669360 (pbk.) | ISBN 9781502669377 (library bound) |
ISBN 9781502669384 (ebook)
Subjects: LCSH: Technology--Egypt--History--To 1500--Juvenile literature. |
Egypt--Civilization--To 332 B.C.--Juvenile literature.
Classification: LCC T27.3.E3 L69 2024 | DDC 609.32--dc23

CPSIA compliance information: Batch #CSCSQ24: For further information contact Cavendish Square Publishing LLC at 1-877-980-4450.

Printed in the United States of America

CONTENTS

INTRODUCTION

The pyramids at Giza are among the largest and most famous examples of ancient building technology anywhere in the world.

The civilization of ancient Egypt lasted for over 3,000 years. During that time, the peoples of the Nile Valley made huge advances in science and technology. They discovered how to build smooth-sided pyramids and how to preserve the bodies of the dead. They understood how to make best use of the flooding of the Nile River to improve farming, and they used math and astronomy to calculate the best times of the year to plant crops. Technology often develops in a series of small steps, rather than in great leaps, and the ancient Egyptians adopted some ideas from earlier peoples such as the Mesopotamians.

KINGDOMS AND DYNASTIES

Egypt was formed around 3100 B.C.E. The king of the Nile Valley conquered the kingdoms of the Nile Delta and unified the country. Egyptian history is usually broken into periods. The Old Kingdom, Middle Kingdom, and New Kingdom were times of relative peace. The country was ruled by pharaohs, or kings, from different dynasties, or families. These times were separated by less stable Intermediate Periods, when dynasties competed for power. This book introduces readers to some of the most important examples of the technology that lay behind Egypt's long history.

This painting shows rowers on an Egyptian boat. The Nile River was Egypt's major highway, and goods and people traveled by boat.

TECHNICAL KNOW-HOW

This early Egyptian pyramid at Saqqara was based on the stepped temples of Mesopotamia.

The earlier peoples in Mesopotamia (present-day Iraq) and Persia (Iran) included the Sumerians, Babylonians, and Assyrians. The ancient Egyptians borrowed, copied, and improved upon knowledge learned from these peoples.

The ancient Egyptians grew plants and kept animals. Most importantly for a desert kingdom, they made full use of the waters of the Nile River. Around 3500 B.C.E. the potter's wheel was invented in Mesopotamia. The wheel for vehicles later developed from this. The Egyptians had little use for vehicles because they had few roads, but the potter's wheel was vital to their civilization. In the same way, cuneiform writing existed in Mesopotamia as early as 2400 B.C.E. The Egyptians copied the idea of writing and created hieroglyphs.

TEMPLE BUILDING

The ziggurat temples of Mesopotamia inspired the pyramids of ancient Egypt. The Egyptians' early attempts to build pyramids ended in failure. The architects did not calculate the size of the base or the angles of the pyramid sides correctly. A number of early pyramids collapsed.

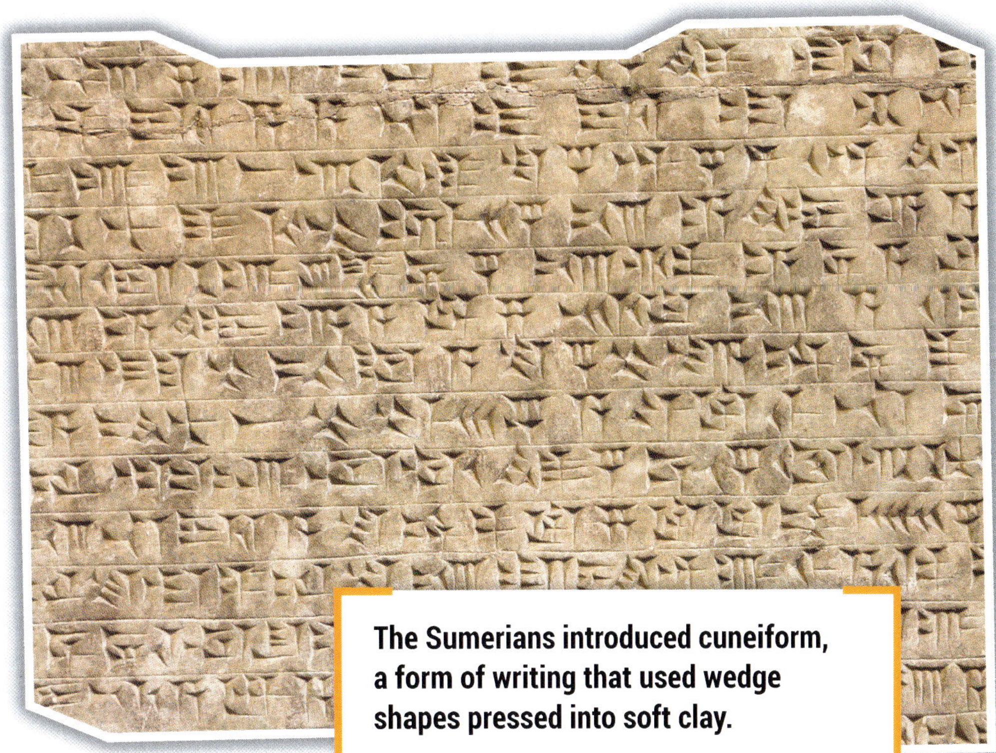

The Sumerians introduced cuneiform, a form of writing that used wedge shapes pressed into soft clay.

The Nile provided the ancient Egyptians with water and a reliable highway for transportation.

THE NILE RIVER

Around 95 percent of Egypt is desert. Its lifeblood is the Nile River, which flows through the country and ends in a large delta emptying into the Mediterranean Sea. Apart from a few oases west of the Nile, Egypt is extremely hot and dry, but the ancient Egyptians built their settlements alongside the banks of the Nile.

Every year the Nile River floods between July and October. The flood leaves a black layer of fertile mud. The rich silt of the Nile meant farmers could grow crops such as barley and wheat. Every year, the flood was different. Too much water and homes were washed away; too little and the crops failed.

ANNUAL FLOOD

To monitor the flood, the Egyptians built nilometers. These were vertical stone columns with regular markings to measure the height of the river. Knowing the height of the flood let the Egyptians plan their annual crop-planting rotations.

TECHNICAL SPECS

» Desert covers more than 90 percent of Egypt.

» The rising waters of the Blue Nile and White Nile caused the annual flooding where they met just north of Khartoum, Sudan.

» Floodwaters spread silt over the land for about 6 miles (10 km) on either side of the river.

» The building of the Aswan Dam in the 1960s finally stopped the annual flooding of the Nile.

» One type of nilometer consisted of a flight of stone steps that led down to the water, such as the one on Elephantine Island in Aswan.

RIVERSIDE SETTLEMENT

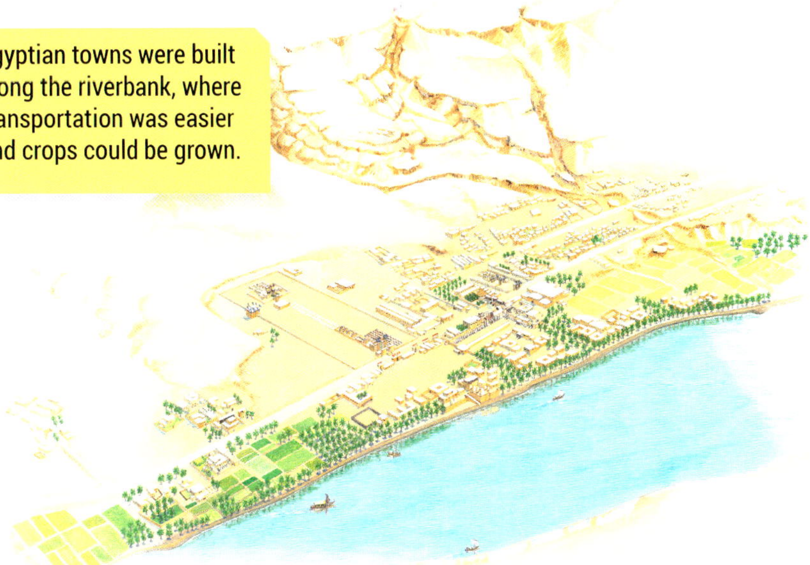

Egyptian towns were built along the riverbank, where transportation was easier and crops could be grown.

FARMING

The Egyptians called the desert the "Red Land." Even surrounded by desert, they were able to grow a surplus of grain on their "Black Land." That made them wealthy. Farming depended on the Nile and its yearly flood, or inundation. The Egyptians also used irrigation to make the land suitable for agriculture.

This tomb painting shows a farmer milking a cow. The Egyptians drank milk and also used it to make butter and cheese.

TYPICAL FARM

Apart from rulers and priests, almost everyone worked on the land. The main crops were emmer wheat and barley. They were made into beer and bread, which were the staples of the diet. Other crops included leeks, onions, beans, figs, melons, and vines. Farmers also grew flax that could be made into linen.

FARMING TOOLS

Farming tools were simple. The soil left by the flood was easy to turn, and plows were pulled by hand or by oxen. At harvest time, grains were cut by hand, using sickles made from wood inset with sharp flint teeth.

TECHNICAL SPECS

» Crops were only planted once a year, after the flood.

» Egyptian farmers divided the year into three seasons.

» Akhet (inundation): From June to September, the Nile flooded and no farming was done. Farmers made or mended their tools, or worked on building projects.

» Peret (growing season): From October to February, the fertile soil left by the flood was plowed and crops were planted.

» Shemu (harvest): From March to May, crops were harvested.

» Women and children worked in the fields and helped harvest the crops each year.

IRRIGATION

Canals were dug to carry river water to more distant fields. Farmers could then use the land beyond the Nile.

Growing crops relies on a good water supply, or irrigation. In ancient Egypt, that depended on understanding the flood cycle of the Nile. Water was stored in large, low-lying areas of land called basins. The Egyptians built canals that took the water to the fields furthest from the river. A device called a shaduf lifted the water from the canal to irrigate the fields.

HOW TO...

The shaduf was based on the lever. A fulcrum was about a fifth of the way along a long pole. The counterweight balanced the weight of the water. A gentle swinging motion turned the pole and emptied the water from the bucket.

The Egyptians constructed huge, flat basins with earth banks next to the Nile to grow their crops. They built a series of gates, or sluices, to divert the river when it was at the peak of its flood. This meant they could trap the water in the basins. The water stayed in the fields for 40 to 60 days before it was drained off at the right moment in the crop-growing cycle.

LIFTING DEVICE

Water was also stored in canals among the fields. To lift water from the canals, farmers used the shaduf. The shaduf was a bucket on a pole with a counterweight. It is still used for irrigation today.

TECHNICAL SPECS

» Nilometers gave farmers early warning of the height of the Nile flood. That meant they could plan how much land to irrigate and prepare the basins.

» The Egyptians adopted the shaduf from the Mesopotamians.

» The flow of floodwater into the basins was controlled by a series of simple sluices, or gates.

» Farmers made sure there was enough water to prevent salts from building up in the fields.

» A steady water flow prevented silting in the canals.

WRITING

A writing system was developed in Egypt around 3000 B.C.E. The first Egyptian writing was hieroglyphs, which were based on pictures. Later, simplified forms of hieroglyphic scripts, hieratic and demotic, were developed for daily use. They were quicker to write than hieroglyphs.

Hieroglyphs were based on pictures. They were used for official purposes, such as inscriptions on monuments.

TECHNICAL SPECS

» Only about 1 percent of Egyptians could read and write.

» Hieroglyphs were carved in stone or painted inside tombs, which is why they have been preserved for centuries.

» Hieratic script ran from right to left. It was written using a reed brush on papyrus.

» Demotic script continued to develop between c.650 B.C.E. and the fifth century C.E.

» In 1799, Jean-Francois Champollion deciphered hieroglyphs on the Rosetta Stone. The stone had the same text in three scripts: Greek, demotic, and hieroglyphs.

This statue shows a scribe at work. Scribes were highly valued in Egyptian society and many held high rank.

Reading and writing was the job of the scribes. All Egyptians of high rank, including pharaohs, trained as scribes. Training took about five years and started as early as age nine. Scribes learned about 700 different hieroglyphic symbols by copying texts. The symbols were pictures that could represent either whole words or individual sounds. Hieroglyphs were carved or painted on monuments, temples, tombs, and religious scrolls.

SIMPLIFIED FORMS

For business and legal documents, letters, and stories, scribes used the hieratic script. The demotic script grew out of the hieratic script around 650 B.C.E. It remained in use for more than 1,000 years.

MEASURING AND MATH

The ancient Egyptians used math calculations to work out how to build their pyramids. The angles relied on accurate measurements and problem-solving. Around 3000 B.C.E. the Egyptians first used numbers that were bigger than 10.

Architects used precise calculations to work out the size of a pyramid's base and the angle of its sides.

The Egyptians used the decimal system of counting that is still in use today. It was likely based on the 10 fingers. There were symbols for decimal units up to one million. They added and multiplied by two. To multiply bigger numbers, they repeatedly doubled or halved, then added the results together.

UNITS OF MEASUREMENT

The Egyptians used the cubit as a measure of length. It was based on the distance from a man's elbow to the end of his middle finger. To measure shorter distances, the cubit was broken into smaller measurements: the smallest was just a finger width. Stretched-out lengths of flax were used as rulers.

TECHNICAL SPECS

» Papyri from 1990–1800 B.C.E. are the earliest evidence of the Egyptians' skill at math.

» A papyrus written in 1650 B.C.E. includes calculations for building a pyramid and shows how to work out fractions.

» The number 1 was depicted by a single stroke; 2 was represented by two strokes, and so on.

» The numbers 10, 100, 1,000, 10,000, and 1,000,000 had their own hieroglyphs.

» The hieroglyph for 100 was a coiled rope; 1,000 was a lotus flower; 10,000 a finger; 100,000 a frog. A million was represented by a god with his hands raised.

CUBIT UNIT

The cubit was based on the distance from a man's elbow to the tip of his middle finger.

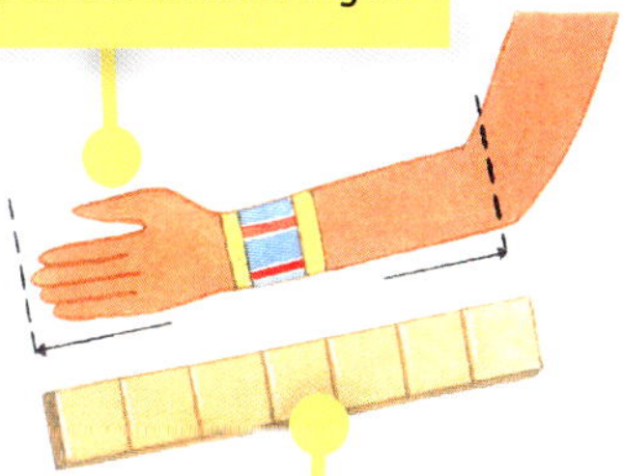

The Egyptians made cubit rulers. Most are just under 21 inches (53 cm) long.

WATERCLOCK

The Egyptians measured time by letting water drip out of a bowl.

PAPYRUS

Papyrus grew widely along the banks of the Nile. It was an all-purpose material for the Egyptians.

One of the greatest technological advances of the Egyptians was the use of papyrus to make paper writing sheets. Papyrus grew all along the banks of the Nile. It was strong and versatile. Its fiber was also used to make baskets, sandals, ropes, boats, mattresses, and even perfume.

MAKING PAPER

The most valuable product of papyrus was paper. The thick green stems of the papyrus were harvested, and the outer fibers were peeled off. The core of the stalk was cut into long, thin strips and then soaked in water to remove the sugar. The strips were laid side by side, with another layer placed on top crosswise. The strips were covered with linen, pounded with weights, and left to dry. Once dried, the linen was removed. The paper was finished by polishing it with a shell or some ivory.

TECHNICAL SPECS

» The younger the papyrus plant, the finer the quality of paper it produced.

» Pens for writing were made from reeds. The end was squashed to make a pointed nib, which was dipped in ink.

» Black was the most common color of ink for official documents. It was made from soot from the bottom of cooking pans mixed with gelatin, gum, and beeswax.

» Different-colored inks were made from minerals that were ground into powder and then mixed with water when used. Ochre was used to make red ink.

HOW TO ...

Turning papyrus into paper was a skilled job. The plant fibers had to be kept damp while they were worked, then dried thoroughly before the paper could be used.

The layers of strips are hammered until they fuse into a sheet, which is then polished

Papyrus is harvested

The stem is cut lengthwise into narrow strips

Two layers of strips are laid at right angles

CONSTRUCTION

The desert had large deposits of limestone, sandstone, and granite, but extracting, cutting, and transporting stone was difficult. Egyptians used stone to build their most important buildings, such as temples, pyramids, and monuments. Ordinary homes were made from simple baked mud bricks.

TYPICAL TOWN

Most Egyptians lived close together in small houses built of mud bricks. They had flat roofs that were used for storage and as workspace. Food was cooked in dome-shaped ovens in open kitchen yards.

Egyptians were experts at quarrying, moving, and using large blocks of stone for their religious buildings.

Among the most important buildings along the Nile River were the huge temples the ancient Egyptians built to honor their gods.

RAISING AN OBELISK

Temples contained many monuments, such as obelisks. Obelisks were four-sided pillars that tapered to a point. Some were very tall. To pull them upright, the builders probably built a large brick-lined pit and filled it with sand. Using rollers and pulleys, the obelisk was tipped into the pit so that its bottom end rested in the sand. Once it was upright, the ramps and funnel were removed.

TECHNICAL SPECS

» To cut limestone slabs, workers hammered wooden wedges into the stone. The wedges were then soaked with water, which made them expand, splitting the rock.

» A brickmaker could make more than 1,000 mud bricks a day. It took five days to make enough bricks for a worker's home.

» Wood was valuable. It was used for doors and window shutters in houses. The most common wood came from the palm tree.

» The Egyptians had toilets but no drains. They emptied their sewage onto fields as fertilizer.

» Stone was transported on barges along the Nile River.

PYRAMIDS

The ancient Egyptians buried their dead rulers beneath pyramids from about 2630 to 1630 B.C.E.

The Great Pyramid of Giza still stands some 4,500 years after it was built. The sides were sloped so that the dead pharaoh could symbolically climb to the heavens, and the shape also represented the rays of the sun. Pyramids were remarkable feats of construction that remained the tallest structures anywhere on Earth for centuries.

The Egyptians built their first pyramid at Saqqara in 2630 B.C.E. They based the shape on the stepped pyramids built earlier in Mesopotamia.

CHALLENGES

Exactly how the pyramids were built remains a mystery. They were aligned on a perfect north–south axis long before the magnetic compass existed. The four sides of the base were always equal in length. Ramps were built next to the pyramid and stone blocks were dragged up on wooden sleds. Blocks at the top were likely put in place by wooden or bronze levers.

TECHNICAL SPECS

» As many as 100,000 workers were used to build the Great Pyramid at Giza.

» The stone blocks weighed up to 15 tons (14 mt). They were marked up in the quarry to show their final position in the pyramid.

» The builders used copper pickaxes and chisels, granite hammers, and other stone tools.

» Pyramids were finished with a layer of limestone on the four sides and gold on the top.

» The Great Pyramid at Giza measures about 755 feet (230 m) on each side. There is only an 8-inch (20 cm) difference between the longest and the shortest sides.

PYRAMIDS AT GIZA

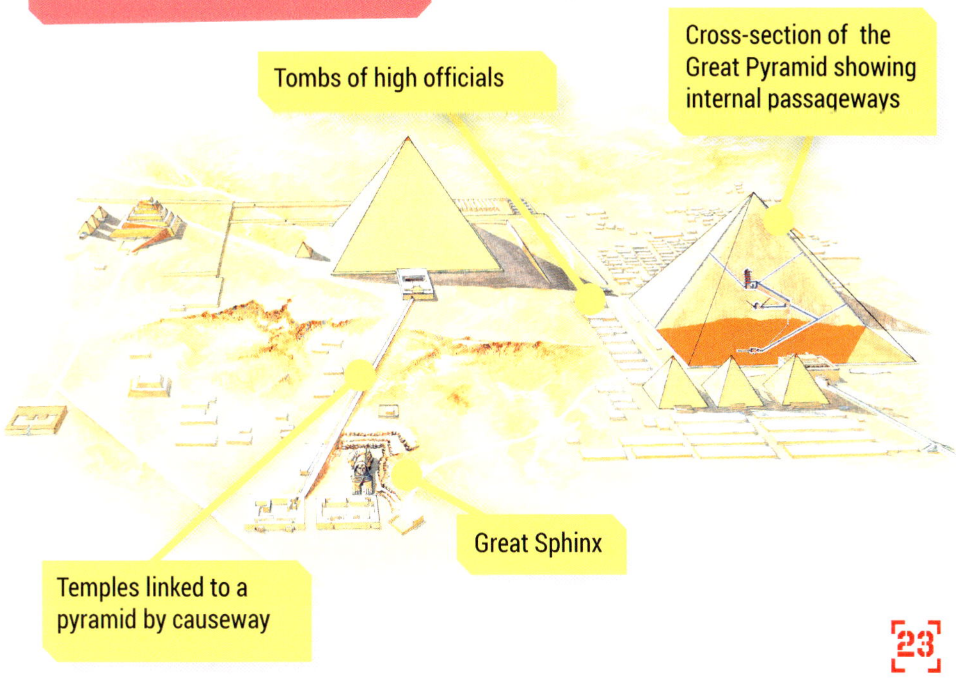

MUMMIFICATION

Mummies were wrapped in linen bandages before being placed inside a coffin. Even animals were sometimes mummified after death.

Preserving the dead through a process called mummification was carried out by a number of ancient peoples. Peruvians also used mummification, for example. However, the ancient Egyptians perfected the method. The process was vital, because the Egyptians believed the body was needed if the person was to live on in the afterlife.

COMPLEX PROCESS

Mummification took thousands of years to perfect. Around 2600 B.C.E., the Egyptians learned that removing the internal organs helped stop the body from rotting. The organs were preserved separately. By 1500 B.C.E., the hollow body and the organs were dried for 40 days in a salt called natron. The skin was sealed with resin, wax, and oil to keep out moisture. The body was stuffed with sawdust and leaves to keep its shape. Then it was wrapped in linen, with protective amulets, or charms, between the layers.

TECHNICAL SPECS

- The earliest Egyptian mummies were buried in hot sand that absorbed the bodily fluids that cause a body to decompose.
- From around 4500–4100 B.C.E., bodies were wrapped in linen soaked in resins.
- Natron is a mixture of sodium carbonate and bicarbonate.
- The organs were preserved in canopic jars.
- The heart was not removed. It had to be weighed by Osiris, the god of the underworld, as the dead person went to the next life.
- The brain and the contents of the skull were removed via the nose using a long, thin hook.

HOW TO ...

Once the body was dried out, it was wrapped in linen. Magic charms were wrapped in the linen to protect the body. The mummy was placed in a coffin and then inside a sarcophagus. The organs were put in containers called canopic jars.

BOATBUILDING

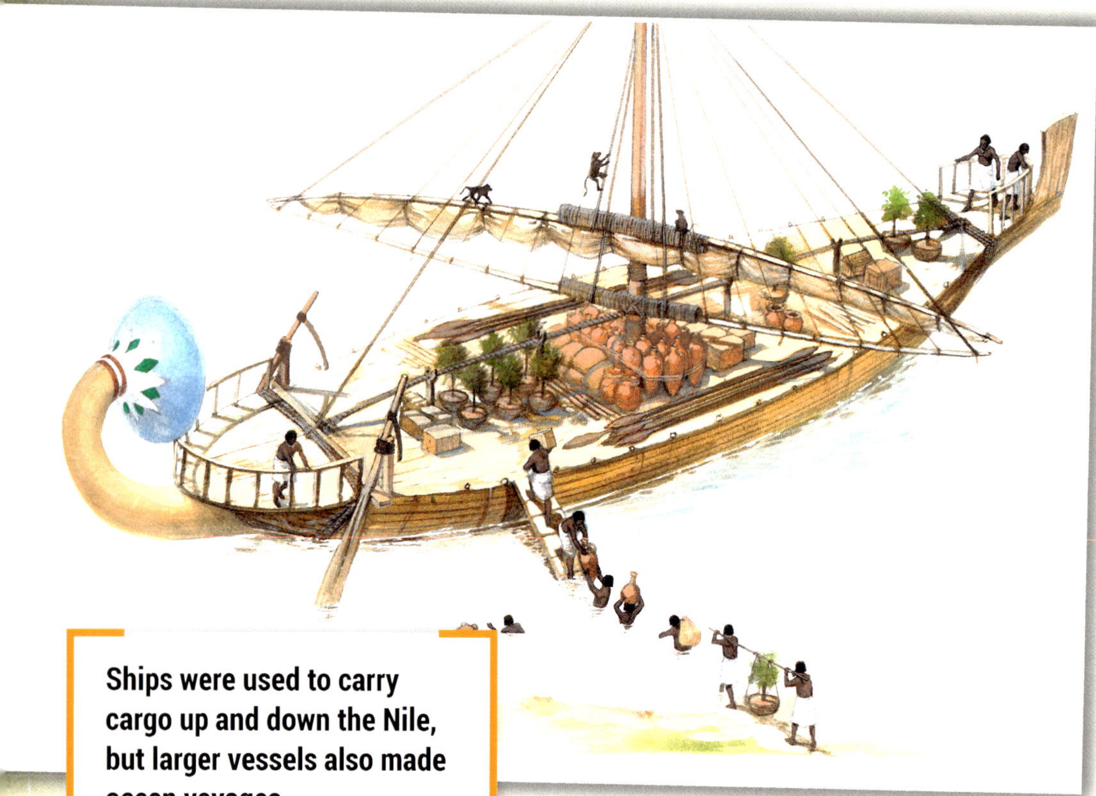

Ships were used to carry cargo up and down the Nile, but larger vessels also made ocean voyages.

Surrounded by deserts and with no roads, the Nile River was ancient Egypt's natural highway. Instead of roads, the river flowed through the country from south to north. Rafts and other vessels were built to transport everything from the huge stones needed to build temples and pyramids to livestock, grain, and passengers.

Egypt lacked trees, so the first ships were rafts made from reeds. These rafts developed into ships with sickle-shaped hulls. Later they had deckhouses and masts with sails. Wooden ships were built from imported acacia or cedar. There were no nails or pegs, so planks were tied together with papyrus.

OCEAN SAILING

Ships had flat hulls to avoid the shifting sandbanks of the Nile. Larger wooden vessels, or feluccas, were capable of sailing in the ocean. They were used to trade with other ancient cultures, such as the Phoenicians, and sailed to the tip of Africa.

TECHNICAL SPECS

» Ships used sails to travel upstream on the Nile and oars and the current to travel back downstream.

» Carpenters lashed together thousands of small wooden planks using ropes of papyrus.

» Boats were sometimes buried near pyramids for the dead to use for transportation.

» The Egyptians built the world's first lighthouse at Alexandria. It was 330 feet (100 m) tall and was visible from 30 miles (50 km) away.

» The heaviest cargo was carried on long, narrow barges towed by other vessels.

NEW KINGDOM BOAT

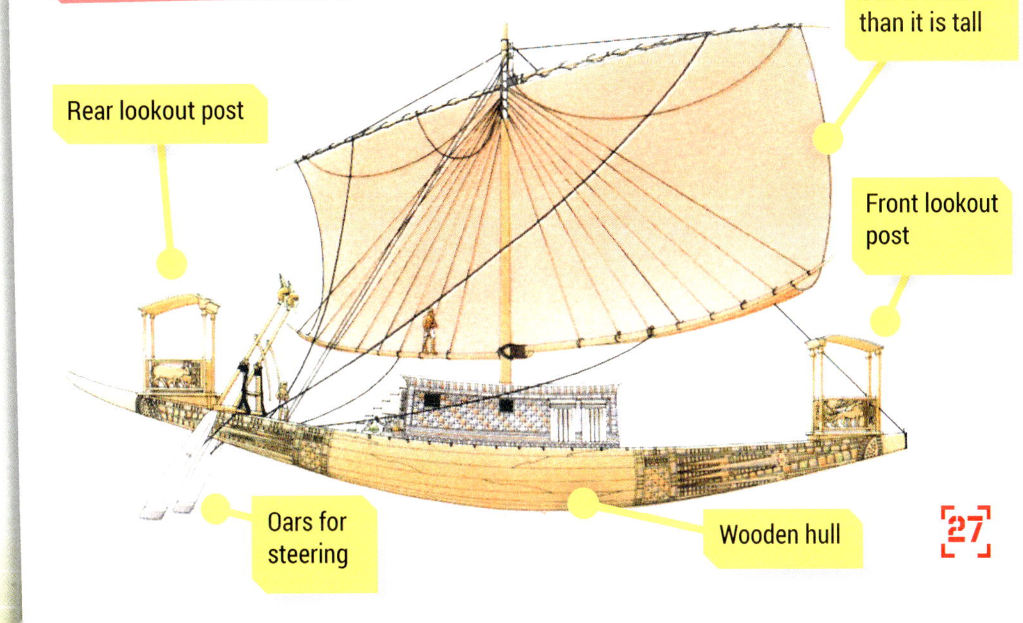

The astronomical ceiling in the temple of Hathor at Dendara shows the gods passing across the night sky.

ASTRONOMY

Many of the important gods of the ancient Egyptians were associated with the stars and planets. By 3000 B.C.E. the Egyptians had started studying the night sky, and priests used detailed maps of the stars during religious ceremonies. A 365-day calendar was developed from observations of the sun.

Astronomers at work. Careful observation of the night sky was the basis of a highly accurate calendar.

Astronomy developed separately in Upper and Lower Egypt before the two kingdoms were united around 3100 B.C.E. In Lower Egypt, astronomers built a circular wall to create a false horizon. On the wall they marked the position of the sun as it rose each dawn. From their observations, they worked out a solar calendar based on a year of 365.25 days.

LUNAR CALENDAR

In Upper Egypt astronomers used a lunar calendar. It was based on the moon and the star Sirius. They noted Sirius rose in a direct line with the sunrise once every 365 days.

TECHNICAL SPECS

- The ancient Egyptians understood the difference between stars and planets.
- They identified five planets: Mars, Saturn, Jupiter, Venus, and Mercury.
- The first recorded date in Egyptian history—4241 B.C.E—was when the Egyptians devised the 365-day calendar.
- The sun god Ra became a major god from 2500 B.C.E. onward. Ra greatly influenced how Egyptians thought about the pharaoh.
- Nut was originally the goddess of the night sky; later she became goddess of the sky in general.

CLOCKS AND CALENDARS

The Egyptians used various devices to tell the time. They measured the length or position of shadows cast by the sun.

As early as 4236 B.C.E. the Egyptians created a calendar based on the cycles of the moon. However, this lunar calendar could not predict when to expect the annual flooding of the Nile. This was the most important event of the year. To do this, priests devised a new calendar. This was based on the movement of the sun.

Priest–astronomers noticed that the Nile usually flooded a few days after the star Sirius appeared in the skies shortly before sunrise. They based a new calendar on the sun, with months based on the cycles of the moon.

DIVIDING THE DAY

The Egyptians divided the day and night into 12 hours each, but the length of an hour varied with the time of year. They invented clocks to measure the passage of time. From 1500 B.C.E. they used sundials to measure shadows cast by the sun. Water clocks were the first timepieces that did not rely on the sun or stars. Water trickled out of a stone jar marked with twelve "hour" sections.

TECHNICAL SPECS

» The ancient Egyptian calendar was made of weeks of 10 days. Three weeks equaled a month (30 days) and four months made a season (120 days).

» Three seasons created a year of 360 days; the remaining five days of the 365-day calendar were feast days.

» To measure the past, the Egyptians used divisions of time based on the reign of their kings.

» The Egyptians were the first people to divide the day into 24 "hours," but they were not of equal length.

» The clepsydra, or water clock, had a small hole in the bottom through which water trickled.

The water clock, or clepsydra, had a tiny hole in the bottom that allowed water to trickle out.

MINING

The famous mask of Tutankhamun, the boy king who reigned from 1333 to 1323 B.C.E., was made from gold with lapis lazuli inlay. Gold and silver vessels, masks, weapons, and ornaments have been found in Egyptian tombs. Gold, silver, and copper occurred as nuggets in rocks, sand, and in riverbeds.

The mask of Tutankhamun was made from gold. It covered the face of the dead mummified king in his tomb.

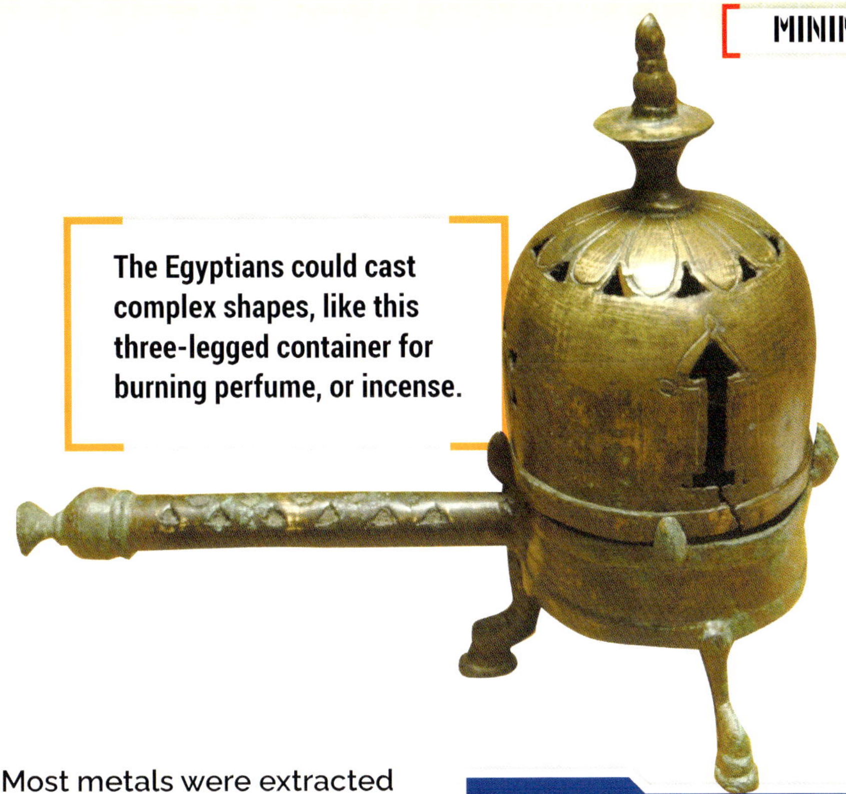

The Egyptians could cast complex shapes, like this three-legged container for burning perfume, or incense.

Most metals were extracted by mining. Underground mining started in Nubia around 1300 B.C.E. Mining was dirty and dangerous, and workers were often slaves.

METAL HISTORY

Gold was widely used, but weapons and tools were made from harder copper. With the invention of bellows around 1500 B.C.E., copper was melted and cast in molds. Imported tin was melted with copper to produce bronze to make weapons, tools, and pots and pans. Once the Egyptians could create higher temperatures in furnaces, they were able to make iron.

TECHNICAL SPECS

» The earliest known map shows the route to a gold mine in the Eastern Desert.

» Metals, mainly copper, were used from 4000 B.C.E. Iron use dates from around 900 B.C.E. While gold was common, iron was rare.

» Copper ore was mined from deserts between the Nile and the Red Sea.

» The Egyptians added carbon to iron to make steel.

» They hardened steel by plunging the hot metal into cold water, then reheated it to toughen it.

MEDICINE

An Egyptian makes an offering to a god. Such offerings were a common response to illness.

Medicine was a new profession in ancient Egypt. Priests first treated patients with prayers to the gods and magic incantations. Early physicians had cures for tumors and eye disorders, and carried out surgical procedures. They wrote their remedies on papyrus scrolls, some of which still survive today.

The ancient Egyptians had an advanced understanding of the human body. Physicians knew that it should be kept clean to prevent infection, as well as making the connection between nutrition and health.

MEDICAL PRACTICES

The earliest known surgery took place in 2750 B.C.E., although no internal surgery was performed. Physicians reset broken bones and dislocated joints. They believed the body was like the Nile; it had channels running through it that carried air, water, and blood. If a person was sick, it meant that the channel was blocked and needed to be unblocked.

TECHNICAL SPECS

- » Amulets were worn as protective charms to ward off illness.
- » Bronze surgical knives have been found, but were probably only used in the mummification process and not for surgery.
- » The Egyptians understood that the pulse and heart were linked. They believed that thinking took place in the heart.
- » The Egyptians knew the position of the vital organs from their treatment of dead bodies.
- » Imhotep, an adviser to King Djoser (2630–2611 B.C.E.), was one of the first physicians and became the god of medicine.
- » Dentistry began in around 2650 B.C.E. Grain and sand in bread soon ground down teeth, so toothache and gum disease were common problems for the ancient Egyptians.

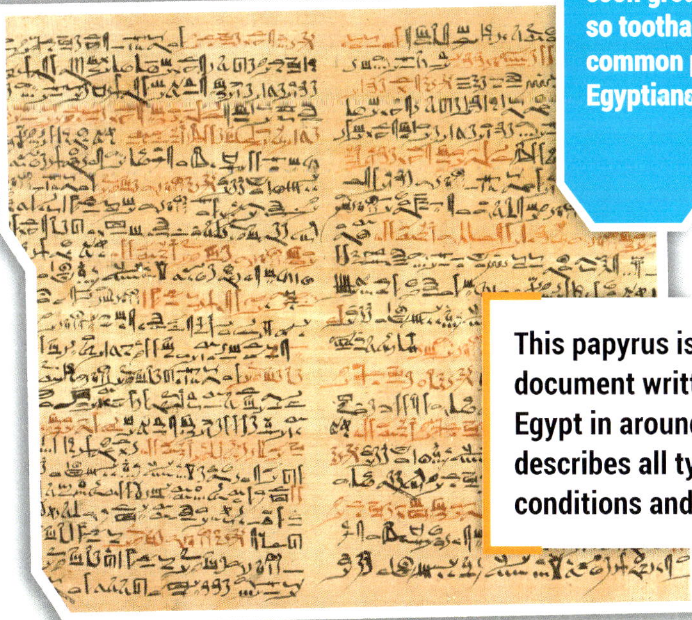

This papyrus is part of a document written in ancient Egypt in around 1600 B.C.E. It describes all types of medical conditions and treatments.

WEAVING AND DYEING CLOTH

As well as grain crops, Egyptian farmers grew flax. This was used to make linen for clothing. Converting the flax plant into linen was a long process. Threads of flax were woven on looms. The earliest known picture of a loom dates to around 3000 B.C.E. Linen was dyed using different minerals to make an array of colors.

The fibers of the flax plant were wound into threads, then woven to make linen.

HOW TO...

The vertical loom replaced the horizontal loom for weaving in the New Kingdom. A wooden frame supported the threads, which were tied with weights to keep them taut. The cross-thread was pushed back and forth between the vertical threads, then pushed up into place.

Flax plants were collected in bundles and soaked in water to break down the tough outer parts of the plant. It was beaten with wooden mallets to separate the fibers, which were spun on sticks (spindles). The spindle had a weighted circular whorl on one end. The spinner set the spindles spinning on the ground. This pulled the fiber from the flax and twisted the thread around the spindle. It was now ready for weaving.

DYEING

Dyes were made from various minerals. Red came from iron oxide or ochre, pale blue from copper carbonate, and green from malachite.

TECHNICAL SPECS

» The weaving of cloth dates back approximately 7,000 years.

» The earliest looms were horizontal. Pegs were hammered into the ground to make a rectangular frame fitted with crossbars to hold the threads. The weaver crouched on the ground to work the loom.

» The vertical upright loom was introduced around 1500 B.C.E.

» People of high rank and the rich wore the finest linen.

» The finest linen was almost transparent; it was only worn by the pharaohs.

» Wool was also widely used to make fabric and wool clothes.

GLASS

By 4000 B.C.E., the ancient Egyptians had learned how to mix natron with sand and the mineral malachite to make a green-colored glass. They called glass *aat wedhet*, which means the "stone that flows." Glass was made into decorative containers and replaced semiprecious stones as beads in jewelry. Because it was highly valued, it was mainly for people of high rank.

These rods of colored glass were found during the excavation of a glassmaker's workshop.

This glass jar held kohl, which was used as eye makeup. Its rich blue color comes from cobalt.

TECHNICAL SPECS

» When sand and natron were heated and became liquid, dirt sank to the bottom and froth rose to the top. When the liquid had cooled and hardened, the dirt and froth were broken off. What was left was the glass.

» Different minerals were added to make color: tin oxide for white, cobalt for dark blue, antimony for yellow, and copper for green.

» To make round beads, the glass paste was coated onto strong thread and formed into a bead shape. The thread burned away in the kiln, leaving each bead with a hole for threading.

» Egyptian glass was heated to 1,470°F (800°C). Today, pure silica is heated to 3,090°F (1,700°C).

The ancient Egyptians first made glass by accident. They ground a mixture of alkali and silica into a powder, which they mixed with water to make a paint. This was then brushed onto a soft stone, called steatite, and then heated until it turned into a shiny glaze that was turquoise in color. It was only around 1450 B.C.E. that glassmakers from Syria showed the Egyptians that this glaze was glass and could be used in many ways.

USING GLASS

The Syrians showed the Egyptians how to shape glass. First they made a clay mold, which was attached to a metal rod. Layers of glass were built up around the mold. It was rolled on a stone slab to make the surface smooth. Once it had cooled, the clay core was removed and an empty glass vessel remained.

POTTERY

Containers of all kinds were used to store food and drink. Vessels were also made to eat and drink from. Such everyday items were made from clay and either hand built or thrown on the potter's wheel. Later a material called faience became widely used for special, decorative objects and was used for vessels and tiles.

When the Egyptians began making pottery plates and bowls some 5,000 years ago, they molded clay around shaped pieces of wood and left it to dry. They did not develop the potter's wheel until a few centuries later. The earliest form of the potter's wheel was relatively slow and turned by hand.

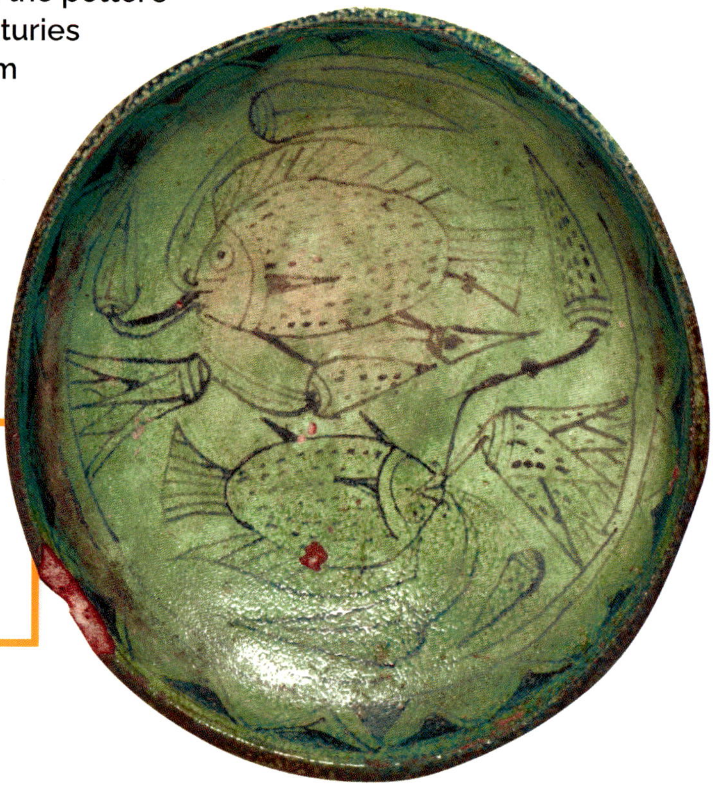

This glazed pottery bowl is decorated with images of fish and lotus flowers.

Around 3000 B.C.E. the Egyptians invented a faster wheel. It worked by using the energy—momentum—stored in a rotating stone wheel. The wheel was wound up and charged with energy by kicking it or pushing it with a stick.

THROWING A POT

The fast wheel enabled a new type of pottery: a "thrown" pot. A lump of clay was put on the rotating wheel and then worked into the shape of a vessel with thin walls. The finished pot was fired in a kiln at a high temperature to make it watertight.

TECHNICAL SPECS

» The potter's wheel was a horizontal spinning disk. It was probably invented in Mesopotamia.

» The kiln was invented by the ancient Chinese. It was first used in Egypt around 5,000 years ago. Pots could be fired at much higher temperatures than if they were simply left to dry in the sun.

» Faience was a type of ceramic made from crushed quartz or sand with a small amount of lime or ash. Water was added to make a paste, which was then shaped. The Egyptians usually added a blue-green color glaze to faience.

Early Egyptian pots such as this lidded jar were made from coils of soft clay that were rolled and smoothed together.

WARFARE AND WEAPONS

The most important weapons in ancient Egypt were the bow and arrow. Around 1800 B.C.E., the Hyksos people from Asia invaded Egypt, bringing horses, the chariot, and a new kind of bow, all of which were adopted by the Eygptians. During the New Kingdom (c. 1550–1069 B.C.E), the Egyptian army consisted of infantry and chariotry.

CHARIOT CHARGE

The chariot and the composite bow were both introduced to Egypt by the Hyksos people. An archer rode on the platform of the chariot with the charioteer. The lack of space meant he needed a shorter bow than ordinary soldiers used. Using a composite bow, he could generate the same amount of power from a shorter weapon.

The army of Pharaoh Ramses II in camp. A chariot is repaired as the infantry stand nearby.

The Egyptian bow could shoot up to 625 feet (190 m). The composite bow of the Hyksos people could shoot a further 260 feet (80 m). The composite bow was made from layers of wood, horn, and animal sinew. Arrows were made of reed with flint heads; copper heads were used from around 2000 B.C.E.

CHARIOTS

The chariot probably originated in Syria. The Egyptians made the vehicle lighter and quicker. The charioteer and an archer stood on a wooden platform at the back, pulled by horses.

TECHNICAL SPECS

» During the first dynasty of the New Kingdom the Egyptian army consisted of infantry and chariotry.

» Chariots were made from wood and leather and pulled by two horses. One soldier drove the chariot, while an archer fired arrows from his bow.

» Chariot wheel rims were covered with leather.

» Egyptian armor was made from leather and bronze.

» As technology improved, daggers were made from bronze and copper.

» The composite bow was given more tension by being bent backward as it was strung.

TIMELINE

B.C.E.

c.5000 The Predynastic Period begins in Egypt.

4241 Egyptian astronomers begin the first calendar.

c.3700 Egyptians learn to extract copper from ore by smelting it in furnaces. The copper is used to make tools.

c.3500 Farmers use plows pulled by cattle to prepare fields so they can plant barley and wheat.

c.3100 King Menes of Upper Egypt conquers Lower Egypt, unifying the country and beginning the Archaic Period.

c.3000 Papyrus made from reeds is used as a surface for writing.

c.2700 Egypt's bronze age begins as smiths learn how to make bronze.

c.2649 The Old Kingdom begins.

c.2630 The first Egyptian step pyramid is built for King Djoser.

c.2600 Bodies have their organs removed and are dried in natron before they are turned into mummies.

c.2590 The Great Pyramid at Giza is built for the Pharaoh Khufu.

c.2500 The Egyptians develop a system of sluices and canals to control the floodwaters of the Nile.

c.2400 An Egyptian artist paints an image of a potter's wheel in use.

c.2150 The First Intermediate Period begins; it is a period of relative instability.

c.2040 The Middle Kingdom begins.

c.1880 Another painting shows a bellows being used to increase the temperature of a fire being used to melt metal.

c.1674 The Hyksos introduce the chariot and compound bow to Egypt.

c.1674	The Hyksos people of the Middle East conquer much of Egypt.
c.1640	The Second Intermediate Period begins.
c.1580	King Ahmose I drives the Hyksos out of Egypt.
c.1555	The shaduf is introduced along the Nile for raising water.
c. 1550	The New Kingdom begins; it marks the strongest period of the Egyptian Empire.
c.1500	Weavers begin using vertical looms.
c.1490	Egyptians begin to make glass vessels.
c.1450	Water clocks are used to tell the time.
c.1200	Iron begins to replace bronze in tools and weapons.
c.1150	The earliest surviving map is created. It shows the location of gold mines in the desert.
c.1069	The Third Intermediate Period begins.
c.664	The Late Period of Egyptian history begins.
c.600	Egyptian ships sail around the continent of Africa.
c.332	Alexander the Great occupies Egypt, beginning a period of Greek rule.
280	The world's first lighthouse is built at Alexandria.
197	A decree by the ruler Ptolemy V is inscribed on stone in Greek and two forms of Egyptian. This Rosetta Stone will allow hieroglyphics to be deciphered in the early 19th century.
30	Egypt is conquered by the Romans.

GLOSSARY

afterlife The place where Egyptians believed the dead went to live.

amulet An object used as a charm for protection against evil.

canopic jar A jar with an animal head used to hold the organs of a mummy.

chariot A horse-drawn, two-wheeled war vehicle with a platform at the back for an archer.

composite bow A bow made from fused layers of wood, bone, and sinew for additional power.

inundation The annual flooding of the Nile.

felucca A fast-sailing ship on the Nile, with a triangular lateen sail.

flax A plant whose fibers are used to make a textile called linen.

furnace An oven that generates high temperatures to melt metal.

hieroglyphs A writing system using pictorial symbols.

infantry Soldiers trained to march and fight on foot.

irrigation A system of artificially watering fields.

kiln An oven used to harden pottery or bake bricks.

loom A frame for weaving yarns to make textiles.

mummy A dead body that has been preserved and prepared for burial.

ore Rocks and minerals in which metals naturally occur.

papyrus A reed whose fibers were used to make paper, also called papyrus.

pharaoh The title given to Egypt's kings and queens.

pyramid A four-sided structure with a square base that tapers to a point.

scribe A person who copies out documents.

smelt To extract metals by heating their ores.

staple A food that makes up the major part of a diet.

FURTHER RESOURCES

BOOKS

Hanovich, Nancy. *1,000 Facts About Ancient Egypt.* National Geographic Kids, 2019.

Kenney, Karen Latchana. *Mysteries of the Egyptian Pyramids* (Alternator Books). Lerner Publications, 2017.

National Geographic Kids. *Everything Ancient Egypt.* Collins Educational, 2018.

Newland, Sonya. *The Genius of the Ancient Egyptians* (Innovations from Past Civilizations). Crabtree Publishing, 2020.

Vallepur, Shalini. *People Did What in Ancient Egypt?* Crabtree Publishing, 2020.

WEBSITES

www.ducksters.com/history/ancient_egypt/inventions_and_technology.php
Ducksters pages on ancient Egyptian science and culture.

discoveringegypt.com/ancient-egyptian-inventions/
Pages on the inventions that came out of ancient Egypt.

www.bbc.co.uk/history/ancient/egyptians/
BBC site that presents an introduction to ancient Egypt.

egypt.mrdonn.org/pyramids.html
Pages about the pyramids on Mr. Donn's social studies site.

Publisher's note to educators and parents: Our editors have carefully reviewed these websites to ensure that they are suitable for students. Many websites change frequently, however, and we cannot guarantee that a site's future contents will continue to meet our high standards of quality and educational value. Be advised that students should be closely supervised whenever they access the Internet.

INDEX